Crazy CREATIONS

Games n' Stuff

Games n' Stuff
First published in 2008 by Hinkler Books Pty Ltd
45–55 Fairchild Street
Heatherton Victoria 3202 Australia
www.hinklerbooks.com

HINKLER
BOOKS

Cover Design: Diana Vlad
Internal Design: Michael Raz
Illustrations: Katie McCormick
Text: Liz Connolly
Projects created by Katrina Meletopoulo
Photography: Stuart Bowey/Ad-Libitum

Thank you to all the children who modelled for the photographs: Alexandra, Anja,
Anthony, Avalon, Caroline, Chloe, Christopher, Dechen, Edward, Elliot, Fabian,
Greta, Heide-Jo, Jack, Jessica, Lyndon, Marlon, Michael, Nayibe, Nicola, Pasang,
Ruby, Ryan, Scott, Stephanie and Xavier.

Printed and bound in China

4 6 8 10 9 7 5 3
09 11 13 12 10

ISBN 978 1 7418 2131 4

CONTENTS

Getting Started

This book contains a selection of great game ideas. Some of the games are simple and easy, while others involve a bit of preparation and creative work.

You can follow the activities in this book step-by-step, or use them as ideas for games of your own!

Games are all about having fun, so make sure that everyone involved in the game feels comfortable and understands the rules.

Some games in this book are more difficult than others, so make sure you choose the right level for you, and if you don't understand something, don't be shy to ask someone to explain.

Equipment

Some basic equipment is always handy to have when you are starting out. Useful pieces include: glue stick, poster paints, paintbrushes, scissors, sticky tape, hole-puncher, crayons, pens, pencils and coloured markers. These things can all be found in the supermarket, but don't worry if you don't have them—you can always improvise with what you've got!

Saving all sorts of stuff for recycling gives you a great choice of unusual materials.

All these materials can be bought in craft shops.

Care and Consideration

Some of these activities involve making a mess. To avoid angry outbursts from your family members, make sure you clean up after yourself. You can protect work surfaces from spills and stains by laying down lots of newspaper or a plastic mat before starting a project.

Buy some good-quality glue for your craft projects. A glue stick (left) is only for gluing cardboard and paper. PVA glue (left) is stronger and dries clear.

poster paint and watercolours

The yellow 'what you need' boxes are next to every craft project, to let you know which items to gather together before starting.

WHAT YOU NEED

- Rubber gloves
- Bowl for bleach
- ! Household bleach
- Biscuit cutters
- Coloured crêpe paper or tissue paper

Important Safety Note

Always take great care when you are handling dangerous tools and poisonous substances. Whenever you see the safety signal ! in the yellow 'what you need' box, ask an adult to supervise you or help with the activity. Make sure you follow the safety tips that appear throughout the book and relate to specific projects.

Board Games

Playing board games on holidays is a great way to include everyone in the fun and to test your skills. They are also handy because they pack flat and don't take up much room.

Neighbourhood Game

Draw the streets and landmarks in your neighbourhood onto a piece of cardboard, then use a toy car to count along the squares of the road to get from start to finish. Add question marks on the occasional square, then pick up a question card to find out whether you have to move forward or back.

WHAT YOU NEED

- Cardboard
- Coloured felt pens, pencils or crayons
- Toy cars
- Die (the plural is dice)

Make a die out of cardboard, as shown. Push a wooden skewer through the middle and spin it like a top.

Make some question cards, too. Think of funny things, such as 'You bumped into an alien at the supermarket. Go back two spaces'.

Take turns at rolling the die, to see how many spaces you drive through. Beep, beep!

First one to the finish wins!

Flower Checkers

This game is also for two players. Each player picks their flower colour, then places the five flowers on alternating squares of the board. The point of the game is to capture your opponent's flowers by jumping over them. Watch out!

WHAT YOU NEED

- Coloured felt
- Scissors and cardboard
- Poster paints
- Paintbrush
- PVA glue or fabric glue

1 Cut paper into 5-cm (2-in) wide strips. Weave the strips in and out of each other to make a board. Glue underneath each strip to hold.

Try to keep your flowers together as you move into the middle of the board.

2 Cut flower shapes out of two different colours of felt and decorate them with poster paints. Allow to dry, then play!

Move your flowers forward by jumping in a sideways or diagonal direction. No cheating!

Set up your checkerboard as we have done here.

WHAT YOU NEED

- Wooden shapes (craft shop)
- Scissors and cardboard
- PVA glue and felt
- Self-adhesive velcro

Hearts and Stars

Glue felt over a cardboard square, to fit snugly. Stick a square grid over the dark background. Paint the stars and hearts, then attach a piece of velcro to the back of each of them, to grip onto the felt board. To win, either player has to get three hearts or stars in a row, in any direction, just like noughts and crosses.

Ball Games to Make

When you have the room to move, or rather throw, ball games are a brilliant way to let loose and really feel the freedom of being active. It's a lot of fun to make up ball games, whether you're playing alone or with friends.

WHAT YOU NEED

- Long sock
- Tennis ball
- Scissors

Sock Ball

This is an incredibly easy thing to make and it's guaranteed to put a smile on your face. When you swing the loose end of the sock over your head before throwing, it really gives the ball some steam. See who throws furthest. Watch it fly!

Throw it, bounce it, swing it and catch it. You can have lots of fun with a sock ball, but don't expect the dog to play fair!

1 First make sure the sock doesn't have a hole in it! Then, push a tennis ball right down into the toe of the sock.

2 Next, tie a secure knot above the tennis ball, to keep it captured in the sock. Cut little snips at the top to make a fringe.

Rubber Band Ball

Super balls are very small, dense balls made from a kind of rubbery plastic. They bounce very high and can be extremely hard to catch a hold of! Make a rubber band ball by wrapping rubber bands around a small bouncy ball. Gradually, the ball will grow until it is the size you want. Try it out for bounce.

WHAT YOU NEED

- Bouncy ball (toy shop)
- Loads of elastic bands in varying sizes

- Cardboard box
- ! Craft knife
- Poster paints or felt-tip pens to decorate box
- Marbles

Make a Marble Run

Turn a shoe box or a small cardboard box upside-down and cut out five archways for marbles to run under. Paint or decorate your marble run and number each archway so that you can keep a track of points earned each time a marble is rolled under an arch. Each person has ten goes at rolling. Tally up at the end to see who's the winner.

Ask an adult for help when using the craft knife to cut out archways.

Stand about 2 m (6 ft) away to throw the ball.

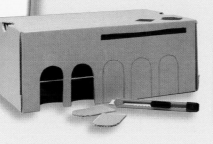

Clown Face

Create a carnival while you're on holidays, whether it's at home during the school holidays or at a more exotic location. Paint a cardboard box and cut out a mouth with a craft knife, wide enough for a ball to pass through. Keep your eye on the ball, or should you keep your eye on the mouth? Whichever, this is a bit easier than those carnival clowns because this one's head doesn't move. Keep a count of how many times you pot the ball. The highest score wins.

Paint on some clown eyes and a wide-open mouth to catch the ball.

WHAT YOU NEED

- Square plastic bin or something stable to raise the box up
- Cardboard box
- ! Craft knife
- Poster paints
- Small ball

Juggling

Perfect your juggling act by making these balls to practice with. If you've ever tried to juggle two or more balls, or anything really, you'll know that it looks much easier than it is!

WHAT YOU NEED

- Coloured balloons
- 1/3 cup raw rice
- Small plastic bag
- Bowl and teaspoon
- Scissors

Balloon Balls

These balloon balls are perfect for juggling because they are light and look fantastic in all their colourful splendour. They are simple to make, but the rice needs to be packed into the bag firmly before you start out.

1 Cut the ends off three balloons. Fill a small plastic bag with the correct amount of rice. Tie off the bag.

2 Pull the first cut-off balloon over the bag of rice to cover snugly. You may have to stretch it to cover the bag.

3 Pull the second balloon over the first and snip it once or twice, so that the first colour shows through.

4 Then, pull over the third balloon and also make a couple of tiny snips. They will widen when stretched.

Watch Me!

Two Balls

Throw up the green ball in one hand and when it's on its way down, throw up the orange ball in your other hand. Alternate hands to keep the balls revolving in a circular motion.

Three Balls

1 Start out with two balls in one hand and one in the other. Throw up the orange ball and catch it in the opposite hand as you throw up the green ball.

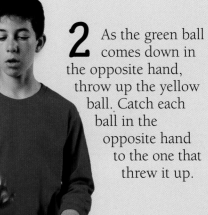

2 As the green ball comes down in the opposite hand, throw up the yellow ball. Catch each ball in the opposite hand to the one that threw it up.

Catch-a-Ball

You'll need to have your eye-hand coordination in tune for this game, not to mention your ball skills. It's the sort of pastime that you can enjoy on your own or as part of a game with a friend. You could take turns to see who can catch the ball in the carton the most times.

WHAT YOU NEED

- Plastic milk or juice carton
- ! Craft knife
- Poster paints
- Paintbrush
- String
- Ping-pong ball

1 Ask an adult to help cut the bottom portion off an empty carton. Paint the carton to decorate. Allow it to dry.

2 Punch a hole in the long end of the carton and thread string through. Attach a ping-pong ball to the end of the string.

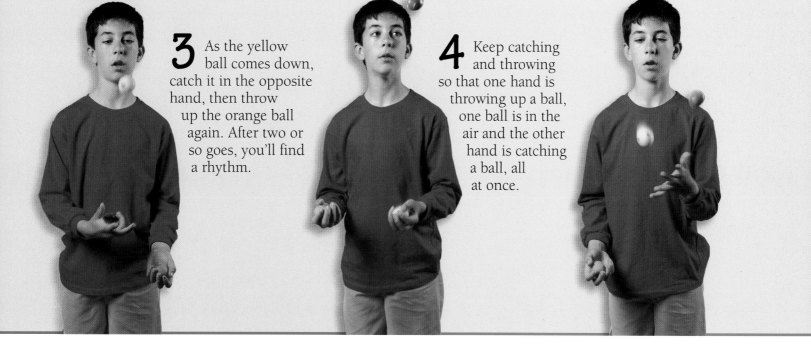

3 As the yellow ball comes down, catch it in the opposite hand, then throw up the orange ball again. After two or so goes, you'll find a rhythm.

4 Keep catching and throwing so that one hand is throwing up a ball, one ball is in the air and the other hand is catching a ball, all at once.

Warm-up Games

If you are having a party, it's a good idea to think up a few games to play at the beginning, to get everyone warmed up and in the mood for some fun. If you are inviting friends from school, as well as cousins or friends who live outside your area, they may not all know each other, so warm-up games are a great way to get everyone joining in the fun together.

WHAT YOU NEED

- Written assignments
- Envelopes
- Stickers to seal envelopes

Sealed Assignments

Start out by giving each player a top-secret assignment in a sealed envelope. The sorts of assignments might include finding out what the names of everyone's pets are, or what everyone's favourite movie is. Choose assignments that are suitable for the age group at your party. This simple game is about getting acquainted—there are no winners or losers.

Who am I?

Write the names of well-known pairs on sticky notes. Possible pairs are suggested below. Stick a note onto everyone's back or forehead. Start asking each other questions, to find out who you are, then find your perfect match.

WHAT YOU NEED

- Sticky notes
- Pen

Possible Pairs
- Tarzan and Jane
- Mickey and Minnie
- King and Queen
- Fish and chips
- Tweedledum and Tweedledee
- Hansel and Gretel
- Tick and tock

Who's a Gorgeous Baby?

Seeing your friends dribbling and looking into the camera with wide-eyed baby stares will have you all in stitches. Ask everyone to bring a baby photo of themselves to your party and pin the collection up so that everyone gets a good look at them all. Each photo is numbered and everyone is given a piece of paper and a pen to write down names that correspond to the numbers. The best baby-guesser wins.

It's hilarious to see who looks like a 'mini me' and who looks totally different.

Keep a small box aside for storing the photos in, so that when the party is over you can give all the photos back.

Tip

To counteract performance anxiety, suggest that people tell a joke while being videotaped.

Lights, Action, Camera

If you have a video camera at home, you could either videotape your party, or make the video itself a sort of theme. Older kids could try writing a short film script with their friends and use the party as a vehicle for acting out the script. Or, try interviewing your friends as they arrive. Replay the video at the end of the party and give out awards for best actor in a comedy!
The possibilities are endless. Think about it and ask an adult to help with organising a video project.

Circle Games

When you are having a party, circle games are another effective way to get everybody to join in. If the games you choose require a few props, make sure that you collect them together before the party begins, to save time later on. When you make a list of games to play, note which ones need props, to help you get organised.

Chocolate Game

All the players sit in a circle and take turns throwing the die. Whoever throws a six moves into the centre of the circle, puts on a hat, scarf and gloves, and tries to eat the chocolate with a knife and fork.
Keep taking turns throwing the die until another six is thrown, then the person in the centre hands the gear over to the next chocolate eater. Keep going until all of the chocolate has been devoured!

Instead of chocolate, try using another snack, such as big slices of watermelon.

`Six!`

Tip
Adapt the games for the number of people playing them. You need at least four players for each game.

You've got to be quick!

WHAT YOU NEED

- Die (the plural is dice)
- Hat, scarf and gardening gloves
- Plastic picnic plate
- Knife and fork
- Block of chocolate or other snack

Animal, Vegetable, Mineral

This one is an oldie, but a goodie. Everyone sits in a circle and the person who begins starts by calling out either animal, vegetable or mineral, while throwing the beanbag to another person in the circle. If the leader has said 'animal', the person catching has to say the name of an animal before they catch the bag. They then throw it to another player. If they can't think of something to shout out fast enough, or they drop the bag, they're out.

Vegetable!

Carrot!

Make a Beanbag

- Rice or lentils for filling
- Zip-lock plastic bag
- Two squares of fabric
! Needle and thread

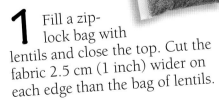

1 Fill a zip-lock bag with lentils and close the top. Cut the fabric 2.5 cm (1 inch) wider on each edge than the bag of lentils.

2 Sew the fabric pieces together on three sides, then slip the bag of lentils inside the fabric bag. Stitch the bag closed.

Try these Circle Games too!

Gone in 60 Seconds
One person stands in the middle of a circle with a stopwatch and says, 'Go' when the stopwatch has been started. Everyone sitting in the circle stands up when they think 1 minute has passed. Whoever stands up closest to the right time is the winner.

Tied in Knots
Everyone stands in a circle and extends their right arm into the circle, then grabs hold of someone else's hand. Then, everyone does the same thing with left hands, too. Next, you have to try to undo the amazing knot of arms in the middle of the circle by stepping over or ducking under people, but without ever letting go of each other's hands!

Happy Hunting

There's nothing quite like being on the hunt for, say, sweets and chocolate! Hunting games raise the excitement levels at parties and clearly identify the super snoops among you.

Treasure Hunts

Hide the treasure, whatever it is, around the garden or in a few rooms of your home and all look for it together. Whoever finds the treasure is allowed to keep it. Or, work in teams with written clues leading you to the treasure, like a treasure map. Divide the spoils among everyone on the team.

Hunt the Button

Hide a variety of old buttons around the house or in your garden before the party begins. Divide into two teams, with one leader in each. When one team finds a button, they shout, 'Hee-haw!' while the other team shouts, 'Moo!' The team leaders are the only ones allowed to pick the buttons up. The team with the most buttons collected after 10 minutes wins.

Hee-haw!

Moo!

Don't get your animal sounds mixed up, or the other team will retrieve the button you've found!

Newspaper Scavenge

For this game, you'll need quite an extensive collection of magazine pages, preferably with lots of headings in large type. The object of the game is to give each player a pair of scissors, a piece of paper and glue, and ask them to cut out and stick down all the letters of the alphabet. The first person to finish wins the game.

WHAT YOU NEED

- A list of assorted everyday items, such as keys, bus ticket, lipstick, feather, red pen, yellow leaf or whatever you like, for each player
- A pen for each player

Tip
Keep a small stock of extra treasure or eats for those who don't find any of their own.

Scavenger Hunts

Make a list of common, everyday items, such as those suggested in the 'what-you-need' box, at left. Hand out a list and a pen to everyone to mark off each item as they find it. The length of the game will depend on how many items can be found, but a short game is probably best. The first one to find most of the items on the list, wins.

Variation

A variation on the standard scavenger hunt is to have the players work in pairs and look for items that begin with each letter of the alphabet, and then to make a list of them. For example, A: animal, aphid or even an angry bee!; B: bark, brussels sprout; C: cat, cauliflower, and so on. Or, to make it quicker and easier, you could ask each pair to list twelve items that all start with different letters.

Music & Dancing

Pump up the volume and show each other what you're made of in the boogie department. Combining music and dancing with a game is a recipe for great fun. There are loads of musical games to play and here are some that are the most fun. You could also adapt the ideas we have suggested, to come up with something more original.

WHAT YOU NEED

- Two broomsticks
- Coloured sticky tape
- Two deep buckets
- Sand
- Bamboo pole
- Hairclips or clothes pegs

Limbo!

How low can you go? With a funky Latin beat and some enthusiastic cheering from friends and family, you can keep on limboing until your limbs go seriously south. Everyone lines up together, and dances to the beat under a bamboo crossbar. If it hits your chin and falls down, you're out. After everyone has had one round of limbo dancing, lower the crossbar for another round and keep lowering it after every round until you have a champion.

The coloured sticky tape on the broomsticks looks decorative, as well as providing measuring marks for lowering the crossbar.

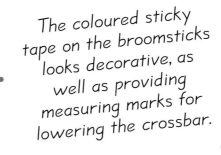

Put the broomsticks into deep, empty buckets, then fill them up with sand to hold them firmly upright.

Bamboo is perfect for using as a limbo pole because it's light and won't hurt anyone when it falls.

A variation of musical islands, for younger children, is statues, where you have to freeze on the spot when the music stops.

Musical Islands

Spread newspaper on the floor, with one less piece than there are players. Dance to the music and when the music stops, leap onto a newspaper island with one hand and one leg touching the paper. Whoever can't stay still, or is left without a paper is out. Remove the same number of islands as children who are out, until the last island is claimed by the winner.

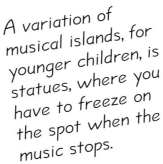

Tip
Make a tape of all your favourite music, so that you don't have to think about what to play during the party.

The hairclips are attached to the broomsticks for the bamboo pole to rest on.

Pass-the-Parcel with Forfeits

Instead of having a little prize or some chocolate between each layer of paper in pass-the-parcel, why not have a note with instructions to stand and sing your favourite song, or recite a poem, rhyme, or whatever! It's much more fun and gets everyone involved. Of course, there's the usual prize at the centre, but perhaps the winner should sing for it first?

Hand Games

If you don't have the space to spread out when playing games, or you don't have the space to pack a lot of equipment into your holiday baggage, think about playing some hand games. They're fun, inventive and more often than not, totally hilarious!

rock

Rock, Paper, Scissors

This game is an old favourite that is often used in making important decisions, such as who will do the washing-up tonight—you or me? Challenge your opponent to a duel of scissors, paper, rock and the best of five wins. It's also not a bad way to decide who has the first turn in board games.

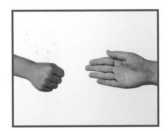
paper

The traditional method is for both parties to shake a closed fist three times before each reveals their 'weapon'.

Paper wraps rock.

Rock blunts scissors.

Scissors cut paper.

scissors

WHAT YOU NEED

- White paper
- Torch
- Limbered-up hands
- Your imagination

Use your imagination and squint a little when the shadow puppet show comes on. You might have to give each other hints, such as animal noises, to help guess.

Shadow Puppets

Shine a torch onto a white background and manipulate your hands and fingers to make a shadow that resembles some kind of bird or an animal.

Whoever is making the shadow keeps the identity of the animal a secret, and then everyone else has to guess what that animal is. All take turns.

WHAT YOU NEED

- Recognisable hand signs
- Animated facial expressions
- An imagination
- Good general knowledge of literature, films, music and television shows

Charades

Charades is a classic guessing game. Take turns at acting out and guessing. When it's your turn to act out, think of a song, name of a TV show, a book or a film, then signal which of those it is by following the guide, below. Then, indicate how many words are in the title, how many syllables in each word, etc, until someone guesses. Let the guessers know when they get a word right, to keep them on track!

four words

second word

two syllables

small word

big word

sounds like...

nearly

right!

TV

book

song

film

Memory Games

Memory games are fun for all ages, but depending on the ages of the children you are playing with, you may want to think about the level of difficulty involved. For example, 'smellies' is better for older children, while the tray game is great for younger kids, too. Be considerate, so that all your friends can join in, whatever their ages. A memory game is a fantastic activity for a rainy day.

You might have to stick the objects onto a tray with plasticine, to hold them up for viewing.

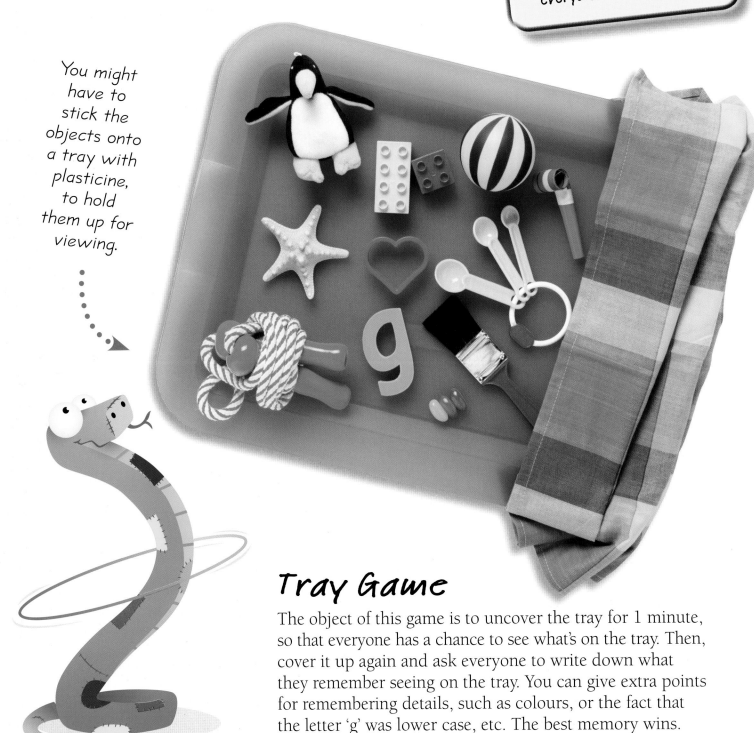

Tray Game

The object of this game is to uncover the tray for 1 minute, so that everyone has a chance to see what's on the tray. Then, cover it up again and ask everyone to write down what they remember seeing on the tray. You can give extra points for remembering details, such as colours, or the fact that the letter 'g' was lower case, etc. The best memory wins.

Smellies

A strong smell is always going to provoke a reaction, and this game is all about some of those nice and not-so-nice smells that make an impression on your memory. It's also very funny to watch the reactions of friends when they take a big sniff of vinegar or curry. Just put a dollop of each smelly substance onto a cotton ball in an empty film canister with a hole in its lid. Make sure that you can't see what's in the canister and discourage impromptu tasting. Best nose wins.

fruit jam

seeded mustard

tomato sauce

curry paste

lemon

ginger

peanut butter

Phoooaaah!

Guess the Sound

This game is about playing a selection of sounds and guessing what they are. It's a good idea to pre-record some sounds, such as ripping paper, brushing shoes, snapping a carrot, pouring water into a bucket or striking a match, to save time. The person who guesses the most, wins.

I Went to a Party...

Sit all of the players in a circle. The first person says, 'I went to a party and wore a hat...' The second person says, 'I went to a party and wore a hat with jewels on it...' And so on, until someone forgets one of the lines, then they're out. The last person to be left reciting is the winner.

Face Painting

- Headband
- Coloured face paints
- Sponge
- Coloured hairspray

Create a new persona for yourself and your friends with face paint. Younger children will need some adult help with face painting at a party, but if you are older, you and your friends could do each other's. Remember to put a bit of moisturiser on under the face paint, to protect delicate skin.

Snake

Try acting the part of a charming snake by having a snake face painted. The full-face coverage will make shedding your skin a bigger job than some of the other designs, but it's fun and different. The green hair looks truly amazing!

These are the basic colours you'll need for making a snake face.

1 Pull your hair off your face with a headband and sponge light green paint all over. Add a darker peaked 'hood' at the top.

2 Paint yellow stripes over your silver eyes. Add a big, dark green line for a smile. The tongue is just a red line with a 'v' shape at the tip, as shown.

Brush your hair back and spray it with green hairspray, being careful to cover your eyes first.

Watch out for that forked tongue!

24

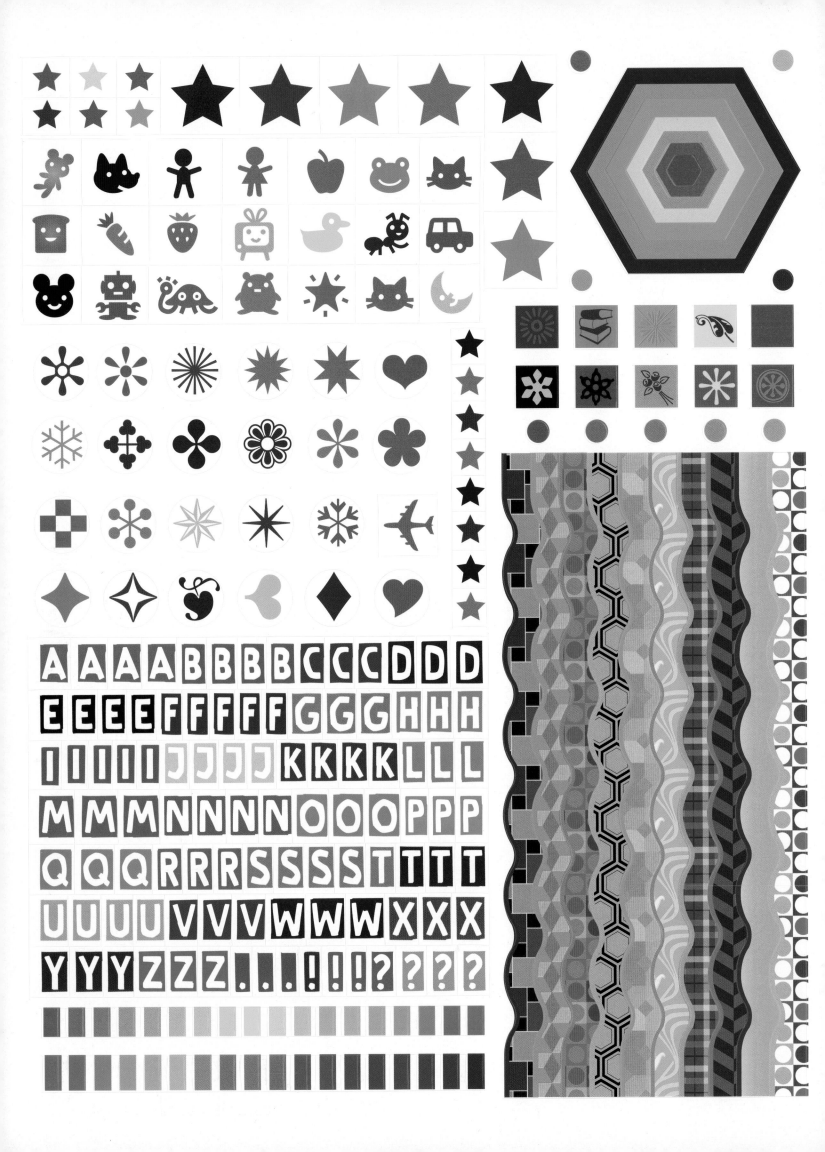

Butterfly

If you've been feeling like a bit of a grub lately, a party could be just the right time to metamorphose into a beautiful butterfly. The butterfly face is colourful and very effective, and the glittering antennae finish off the look nicely. It's also a good choice for smaller children. Another option to consider for smaller kids is a ladybird face.

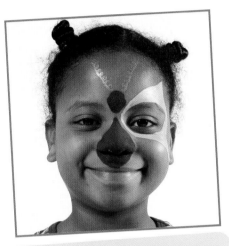

1 Paint the butterfly's body and head. Make gold squiggles for antennae. Add the wings around each eye and decorate, as shown.

2 Wind a pipe cleaner tightly around a pencil. Then, slide it off gently. Glue a pom-pom to the top of the pipe cleaner.

Paint coloured spots on the butterfly's wings, to finish off the look.

Twist the pipe cleaners onto a hard plastic headband.

Line up the pipe-cleaner antennae with the squiggly gold lines painted on your forehead.

Keep a few hair ties handy, for friends who need to tie hair out of the way.

25

Sparkly Face

All that glitters is not gold, said Shakespeare. In this case, the glittering comes from gold, silver and bronze. So if you are partial to a bit of sparkle, this could be the face for you. We have stuck little jewel-like hearts on this face to make the design more interesting. The crowning glory is the fantastic beaming-heart headband. Wear it well.

WHAT YOU NEED

- Headband
- Glittery pipe cleaners
- Face paints (including metallic colours)
- Pre-made foil heart shapes
- PVA glue
- Coloured hairspray

Feel free to experiment with colour and pattern. Make face painting unique and creative!

Make starry patterns with the sparkly stickers.

glittery face paint and shiny hearts

1 Plait three pipe cleaners together to make a headband. Twist pipe cleaners on top, to stand up, as shown.

2 Bend the headband into shape. Glue foil heart shapes to the upstanding pipe cleaners.

3 Paint your face all over with silver, except for your lips and a triangle over your forehead, which are painted bronze.

Robot

The robot is another full-face painting job, so keep a bit of cold cream or make-up remover handy, in case anyone decides that they've had enough of being automated and would like to slip back into their own skin. As with all of our suggestions for face painting, they are just that—suggestions—so don't be afraid to try something different and experiment with your own ideas. For instance, you might like to make a Frankenstein face instead, so all you have to do is find a picture, from a book cover or a magazine, and adapt it to make your own style of monster.

1 With hair pulled back, paint your face silver and blue, as shown. Paint the silver areas first, then the geometric blue bits.

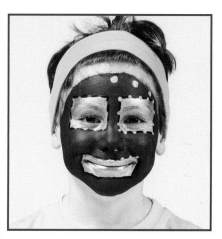

2 Add black lines around your eyes and mouth, then dot yellow on top. Paint slightly larger circles along your forehead.

If you make a mistake, carefully remove your face paint and try again.

Use hairspray outdoors, so that you don't breathe in the fumes. And always remember to cover your eyes.

Don't forget to try out a bit of robot-style conversation, 'A-ffirm-a-tive'.

27

Obstacle Race

This game is a lot of fun and can be played indoors or out, as long as you have enough room. Try to organise all the equipment before the game begins and have a diagram of your obstacle course on hand, so that you or an adult helper can set it up quickly and easily. Make sure that you give the players clear instructions. The one who finishes fastest is the winner.

1 First up, crawl through the tunnel on all fours.

2 Then, throw six balls into a basket or bucket.

3 Put on some dressing-up clothes and skip ten times.

4 Take off the dressing-up clothes and hop through each hoop.

5 Pick up the last hoop and hula like mad ten times.

6 Put a beanbag on your head and crawl backwards to the finishing line.

FINISH!

Wheels on Fire!

This is a perfect outdoor game for older party-goers who are adept at riding bicycles, but you'll also need a bit of adult help and supervision. Firstly, make sure that everyone who plays wears a safety helmet, and that the bicycle is adjusted to the correct height before beginning. The person to finish the course fastest, wins.

1 Firstly, weave in and out of the row of cups without touching any of them.

2 Pick up a hula hoop and throw it over the stool without knocking over the spray bottle.

3 Then, ride past and pick the spray bottle up off the stool.

4 Lastly, 'shoot' the ping-pong balls off the tops of the bottles before riding to the finishing line.

You can vary this game by using a scooter instead.

FINISH!

Eating Games

How hard can it be to eat your way through a game? Pretty hard if it involves no hands! Sometimes an open mouth just isn't enough, so you'll have to come up with a new strategy for getting the food off the string or out of the water and into your mouth. May the most ingenious mouth win!

Apple Bobbing

This is a game that kids have played for generations. Each player has to try to take a bite out of an apple that is bobbing up and down in a water-filled container, without using their hands. Whoever takes the most bites in 1 minute, wins. Playing in groups of three or four works well.

WHAT YOU NEED

- 3 or 4 stools or low chairs
- 3 or 4 medium-depth dishes
- Lots of apples

Tip
Make sure that none of your friends are allergic to any of the food that you serve.

Hanging Apples

This game is a variation on apple bobbing and requires fewer props. Make a hole right through each apple with a skewer, then thread a long piece of string through each hole and secure. One person holds the end of the string while another sits on their knees, hands behind their back, and tries to take a bite out of the apple.

WHAT YOU NEED

- Lots of apples
- String or ribbon
- Wooden skewer

'Hanging apples' is easier to organise by dividing everyone into groups of two. You could all take turns dangling.

Everyone can keep their apple for a healthy snack after the game!

WHAT YOU NEED

- As many doughnuts as there are players
- Broomstick
- Plastic string

Dangling Doughnuts

Tie a piece of string through each doughnut hole and attach the end of it to a broomstick, so that the doughnuts hang down. Line up all the players and when the referee shouts, 'Go!' you all have to try to eat your doughnut, without using your hands. The first to finish wins. Good luck!

Happy eating!

Cinnamon doughnuts cause less mess than iced ones!

You can substitute doughnuts with circular slices of pineapple.

Party Food

Having plenty to eat at your party is pretty important, but not as important as what it is that you eat. After all the games you will have played by the time you're ready to eat, it's a good bet that everyone has had more than enough lollies and chocolate, at least for the time being. Serving food that is both tasty and reasonably nutritious is a first-class way of performing a delicate balancing act.

WHAT YOU NEED

- Tomato paste or purée
- Sliced capsicum rings
- Button mushroom caps
- Stuffed olives
- Salami
- Cherry tomatoes
- Pitted black olives
- Fresh mozzarella
- Bean sprouts
- English muffins or pita

Pizza Heads

These faces are a lot of fun to make together as a party activity and they don't take up heaps of time. Prepare all the ingredients before the party and refrigerate them until you're ready to put faces onto English muffin or pita bread bases. Ask an adult to pre-heat the oven grill to high, then slide the pizza faces under until the cheese has melted. Bon appétit.

Tomato paste can be bought in a packet or jar.

Get a look at this one's hair. It's positively sprouting!

Have some eyebrow-raising fun while you make funny pizza faces at your party.

Organise the ingredients well in advance.

Tip

Keep the party food simple and don't have too many choices on offer. Put some cut-up fruit out, too.

'I've got eyes at the sides of my head!'

Who's a cheeky boy, then?

A small, but perfectly formed, face.

32

Crazy Cup-Cakes

Okay, you've had the pizzas and the sliced fruit, maybe a sandwich or two, so it's back to the sweets. It is a party, after all. You might want to have cup-cakes available for everyone to eat throughout the party, or you could decorate them as another fun thing to do together. Ask your parents or an adult for help with making the cup-cakes, or buy some ready-made.

You can buy pre-packaged tubes of jelly icing from party shops and some supermarkets.

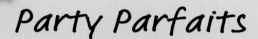

Party Parfaits

Parfaits are frozen desserts that are made up of layers of custard, ice cream, whipped cream and syrup. You can make them in individual cups, or in a bigger bowl that you scoop from, to serve. It's the most delicious dessert and especially good for a summer party, when everyone is hot and sweaty from playing games. Decorate the parfaits with hundreds and thousands or simply squeeze on some chocolate sauce after you've taken them out of the freezer. Yum!

WHAT YOU NEED

- Enough cup-cakes for everyone at the party
- Different coloured icing (just mix icing sugar with a little water or milk to make a smooth paste. Add a few drops of food colouring for your choice of coloured icing)
- Food colouring
- Lollies for decoration
- Pre-packaged tubes of jelly icing for decorating

Team Games

Summon the Olympic spirit and get your cheering calls ready for the team games. There's no better way to drum up the excitement and thrill of a competition than when you're all in it together, pitching the skill and know-how of one group against the other—and may the best team win!

Balloon Relay

Organise yourselves into two teams, with each team standing in line. The first person has to put an inflated balloon between their knees and run, without dropping it, to a designated point before returning and passing the balloon, still between knees, to the next team member. The winning team is the one that finishes the relay first.

Variations

You can vary the relay by passing the balloon over the leader's head to the next person, who passes it under their legs, then they pass it to the next person, who passes it over the their head, and so on, until finished.

It's not easy to run and laugh at the same time, but you can give it a try!

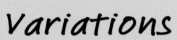

Pass the Matchbox

Decorate a matchbox and remove the inside 'drawer'. Divide into two teams, then start passing the matchbox, on your nose and without using hands, from one person to the next. The first team to finish wins.

WHAT YOU NEED

- Empty matchbox
- Poster paint
- Paintbrush
- Stickers

Pass the Orange

Divide into two teams, each with a team leader. The leader has an orange tucked under their chin and they have to pass it to the next person, and so on, without using hands, until the orange reaches the last person in the line. The first ones to finish, win. An interesting variation is to all sit down and pass the orange with your ankles.

Spoon Threading

With a roll of string in one hand and a spoon tied to the end of the string in the other, start threading the spoon through your T-shirt and down the leg of your pants, so that it comes out at your ankle. Then pass it on to the next person, who threads from the bottom up and then passes it to the next person in line, who threads top to bottom. Keep going until you are all on-line, then try doing the conga!

Tip

A team of about five or six people is best, so have more teams rather than two very big teams.

Don't forget to keep the string on its roll, otherwise you may end up having a piece that's way too short.

More Team Games

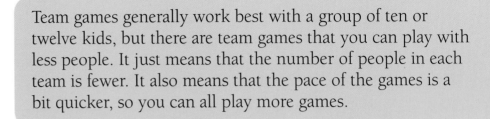

Team games generally work best with a group of ten or twelve kids, but there are team games that you can play with less people. It just means that the number of people in each team is fewer. It also means that the pace of the games is a bit quicker, so you can all play more games.

Curse of the Mummy

Try preserving some of that game spirit with a bit of good old-fashioned mummification. There's no gluing or taping, just endless streams of toilet paper and plenty of giggling.

Each mummy stands with legs and arms apart while they are wrapped from head to foot in toilet paper. An adult helper can time the wrappers and signal when 2 minutes are up. Best mummy wins. At the end, have some fun busting free from your bandages!

Tip

Make sure that you line up all the mummies and take a photo after judging 'best mummy'.

It's a wrap! Work against the clock and see whose mummy is the best after 2 minutes of hard work.

WHAT YOU NEED

- A roll of toilet paper for each person wrapping
- Lots of elbow grease!

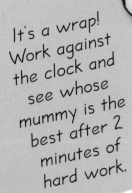

I hope the mummy doesn't put a curse on us!

Each team has one mummy and at least two 'wrappers'.

Make sure there's no skin showing— this mummy is still naked!

36

Lolly Race

Each team member has a straw. The leader sucks up a lolly on the end of their straw and keeps it there while they walk to the end of the room and back again, without using hands. Everybody has a turn until each team has finished. First team to finish is the winner.

You can use jelly beans or round-shaped lollies for this game.

WHAT YOU NEED

- Jelly beans or other suitable lollies
- Plastic drinking straws

Glove Gum

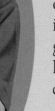

You need to have as many people in a team as there are sticks of gum in a packet. The idea is that the first person in each team puts on the gloves and takes out a piece of gum, unwraps it and pops it into their mouth before taking off the gloves and handing them to the next in line. The first team to have everyone in it chewing away, wins.

WHAT YOU NEED

- Gardening gloves
- Sticks of gum, individually wrapped

37

Outdoor Games

There are loads of games to play outdoors, some with props and some with just a group of people. So, start recruiting and get your friends together to plan which game you'll start with first. The running games don't need special equipment.

Tip

Try to play outdoor games in open, grassy areas to avoid any injuries.

Tip!

This is a game of chasings. Someone is 'It' and everyone else gets chased by them. If you get touched, then you have to stop still until someone crawls under your legs to release you. Choose a safe place, such as a wall or tree, called 'Bar', to go to where 'It' can't touch you. Take turns being 'It'.

Nose Tip

In this variation, to avoid being tipped you have to bend one arm under your knee and touch your nose. Try doing that in a hurry!

Point-to-Point Tip

This game has two 'Bars' at either end of the yard. 'It' has to stand in the middle while everyone else is at one 'Bar'. On the count of three, all run to the other 'Bar'. Whoever gets tipped is 'It'.

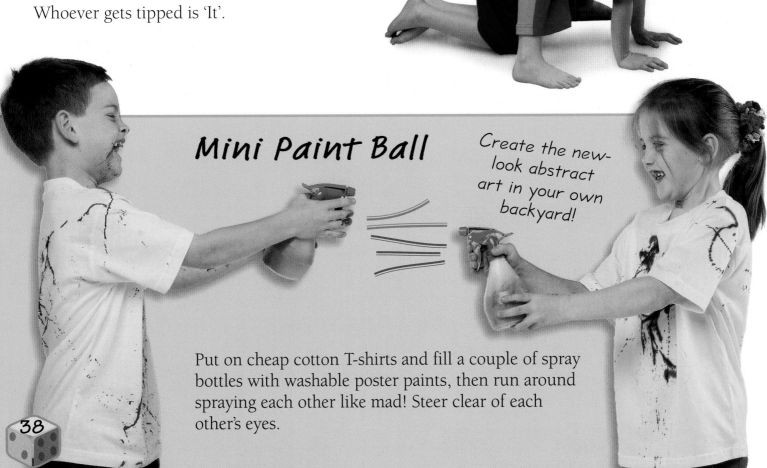

Mini Paint Ball

Create the new-look abstract art in your own backyard!

Put on cheap cotton T-shirts and fill a couple of spray bottles with washable poster paints, then run around spraying each other like mad! Steer clear of each other's eyes.

Walk Tall

Try making these stilts for a bit of fun outdoors with your friends and family. You'll have to try to coordinate your hands and feet to find your rhythm, but then there will be no stopping you. Walking on paths is easier at first than trying to walk on the grass, until you get the hang of it. Either way, enjoy the higher altitude. What's the weather like up there?

WHAT YOU NEED

- Two strong plastic flowerpots
- ! Power drill
- Rope long enough to reach from your hands to your feet, doubled over
- Coloured circle stickers

1 Ask an adult to drill two holes directly opposite one another at the bottom of a flowerpot. Thread rope through to the inside and knot firmly.

2 Thread the other end of the rope through the second hole in the flowerpot. Pull the rope to the inside of the pot and knot that end firmly, too.

3 Decorate the flowerpot with coloured circle stickers at random. Repeat steps 1, 2 and 3 with the other flowerpot so that you have one pot for each foot.

Flowerpot Race

Another great idea is to have a flowerpot race. Get a hold of two empty flowerpots each, stand with one foot on each pot at the starting line, then bend over and use your hands to lift the pots forward, one at a time, with your feet on them until you make it to the finish. You'll soon find out who's coordinated!

Remember to bend your knees up when your arms are lifting up the flowerpot.

If you touch the ground or fall off, you have to start again!

Move the left foot forward, then switch over to the right.

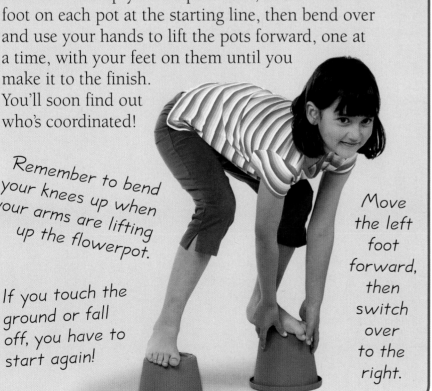

WHAT YOU NEED

Water Games

- Long skipping rope
- A plastic cup filled with water
- At least three players

It's a good idea to wear your swimming costume or an old T-shirt and shorts while you're playing water games. That way you can concentrate on having as much fun and getting as wet as possible without having to worry!

No-Spill Skipping

Everyone lines up to skip rope three times while holding onto a cup full of water. The rope holders keep the rope twirling while each player jumps in for their turn. Whoever has the most water left in their cup after having a few turns is the winner.

Keep your glass away from your face to avoid an unpleasant splash!

Count aloud while you're skipping so that you know when your turn is up.

40

Water-Bomb Battle

Fill the balloons to three-quarters full with water and tie off tightly. Organise yourselves into two teams that face each other. One player on each team has to deflect the water bombs thrown from the other team. Everyone takes at least one turn at deflecting the water bombs. Let chaos rule and all start throwing water bombs at once!

WHAT YOU NEED

- Water-bomb balloons
- Water
- One plastic tray for each team
- Teams of players

Warning: this game can leave you soaking wet!

Tip
Play water games on the grass, to prevent slipping over onto a hard surface.

Water Bomb

Dip an open zip-lock bag into a bucket of water and seal. Then aim it at your target! You can keep refilling.

Swimming Pool Games

Marco Polo

One person is nominated to be 'It' and has to move about in the pool with eyes closed tightly, shouting 'Marco!', while everyone else replies with 'Polo!'. The 'It' person uses the direction of the sound to find and tip another player. Whoever gets tipped is the new 'It'.

Relays

Organise yourselves into teams. The first swimmers dive in and swim a lap of the pool, racing against each other. When they tip the end of the pool, the second swimmers in line jump in and swim a lap, then the third, and so on. Try swimming different strokes, too. You could use a stopwatch to see who's the fastest.

Ball Games

Keep your eye on the ball and get ready for some more games. As long as you have enough room to spread out when you are playing your ball games, and you are not using a hard ball, such as a cricket or softball, you can have a lot of fun. Here are a few quick and easy suggestions.

Down and Out

Toss the ball back and forth to each player and whoever drops the ball has to drop onto one knee. Keep tossing the ball and if the same player drops it a second time, they have to drop onto two knees, then on one elbow, the other elbow, the chin and then they're out!

Bucket!

Lay down a length of rope (up to 10 m [30 ft]). Take turns at trying to throw balls into the bucket at different lengths along the rope, starting from the closest point. Whoever throws a ball into the bucket at the furthest distance along the rope is the winner.

WHAT YOU NEED

- Tennis ball
- Players in a circle

WHAT YOU NEED

- Tennis or rubber balls
- Plastic bucket
- Rope (optional)

Try not to bounce too hard, otherwise the ball will bounce right out of the umbrella.

WHAT YOU NEED

- Tennis or rubber balls
- An open umbrella

Umbrella Bounce

This one is a quirky variation of quoits. Lay down the open umbrella so that it is facing you. Stand about 1 m (3 ft) away and toss the ball so that it bounces once and then lands in the umbrella. The one with the most balls in the umbrella at the end is the winner.

Never take your eyes off the ball, no matter how big it is!

WHAT YOU NEED

- Huge inflatable beach ball
- Strong muscles!

88!

Air Count

The idea is that everyone keeps the ball aloft by hitting it with their hands or clenched fists, one at a time, volley-ball style. All count together each time the ball is knocked back up into the air.

Blanket Toss

Every team needs four people to hold each corner of a blanket. All toss the ball off the blanket to the other team, who toss it back again.

This game makes beach volleyball look really tame. Get coordinated and bounce back!

Tenpin Bowls

Set up about ten empty plastic drink bottles on a flat surface. Everyone has a turn at trying to knock over the pins with a small ball, standing about 6 m (20 ft) away. Each bottle skittled is equal to one point. After everyone has had ten turns, the highest scorer wins.

Line the bottles up in a triangle, with the point facing you.

Fun After Dark

It's a good idea to wear your swimming costume or an old T-shirt and shorts while you're playing water games. That way you can concentrate on having as much fun and getting as wet as possible without having to worry!

Boo! Isn't it weird how everything becomes so much more spooky and scary after dark? You can use that added excitement to your advantage with outdoor games in the dark, whether you're still at home in the backyard, or camping out somewhere more remote. Get your night vision into play and let the after-dark games begin.

WHAT YOU NEED

- Four or more players
- A hiding place

Sardines in the Garden

This is a hiding game where one person goes off to find a hiding place while all the other players count to fifty. Then everyone disperses and goes looking for the person hiding. When each person looking finds the person hiding, they have to stay quiet and squish into the hiding place, until another seeker finds them, then they squish in, too. Keep squishing into the same hiding place until there is nobody left looking and you are all together like sardines in a can!

Scary Story Contest

WHAT YOU NEED

- A torch
- Your best scary face
- An original story
- A horrified audience

Scary creatures, spooky sounds, your story is the best that's found! Well, that's the idea, anyway. You all take turns telling a story or a spooky poem to a suitably horrified audience with the torch positioned under your chin. Make them jump! The best and the scariest storyteller is the winner.

This guy takes his scaring very seriously! Watch out for nightmares and be considerate of little friends who are still too young to be scared.

Light and shadow create amazing changes that can have a pretty dramatic effect. Try alternating faces and use your best weird voice, too.

Creepy Puppets

Shadow puppets are fantastic for creating the right mood or telling a spooky story. These creepy puppets work in the same way, but the shadow is made by black cardboard placed in front of a white background with torchlight shone onto the background. Ask a member of the audience to shine the torch, and let the show begin.

WHAT YOU NEED

- Black cardboard
- ! Craft knife
- Wooden skewers
- Black poster paint
- Sticky tape
- Torch

Ask an adult to help you use a craft knife to cut out the shapes from black cardboard. Tape painted skewers to the back of each puppet.

Flash the torch onto a white background with the puppets up in front of it. Jiggle the puppets up and down for shadow effects.

WHAT YOU NEED

- A torch for each player
- A small group of people
- Hidden treasure, such as chocolate or small prizes

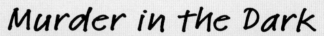

Murder in the Dark

Put as many folded bits of paper as there are people playing into a bowl. All take a bit of paper and the one who has an X marked on theirs is the murderer. Then you all creep about not knowing who the murderer is. The murderer has to draw an X with their finger on everyone else's back without anybody seeing them. If you feel an X marked on your back, you have to lie down dead. Keep playing until the murderer's identity is revealed or everyone is murdered, whichever comes first. You'll start feeling shivers right down your spine!

Torchlight Treasures

A really fun thing to do after dark is to have a treasure hunt. Everybody joining in will need to have a torch, unless you pair up and share the booty. It's just like a regular treasure hunt. Hide the treasure beforehand, then all start doing a bit of detective work until the last of the treasure has been found. Happy hunting.

Travel Games

Have game, will travel. There's only one way to break up the monotony of travelling from one place to another, and that's with a couple of well-chosen travel games. We have come up with an inspired selection of games and ideas that are guaranteed to make your trip a fun one. Happy travelling!

Car Bingo

Before your trip, each cut out a variety of magazine images, like the ones shown below, and stick them onto cardboard. While you are driving along, call out loud if you spot something from your bingo board and mark it off. Whoever finishes their board first, yells 'Bingo!' and wins.

To reuse the board, have it laminated or cover it in contact, so that the non-permanent pen can be wiped off.

Try to be realistic about what you are likely to see from the car when you choose the images.

WHAT YOU NEED

- Lots of magazine images
- Scissors
- PVA glue or glue stick
- Cardboard and contact
- Red white-board marker

- Pack plenty of paper, pens, pencils, a rubber and a pencil sharpener.
- Take an ordinary pack of playing cards for a game of Old Maid, Snap!, or to build a card house.
- A portable CD or tape player is great for music and for talking books.

Use a red pen to mark off the pictures that have been spotted.

- Two players
- Two pens
- Paper

Hangman

Think up a word and write a dash to represent each letter. The other player guesses which letters are in the word. Each time they are wrong, part of a stick man hanging from the gallows is drawn. If they guess your word, they win, but if they are hanged first, then you are the winner.

Association

The first person claps three times and says any word they choose. The second person claps three times then says a word that the first word reminds them of. Keep going until someone can't think of a word or they forget to clap.

Tongue Twisters

Try reciting this quickly: 'She sells sea shells by the seashore, the sea shells she sells are sea shells, I'm sure.' Or, try saying: 'Red leather, yellow leather', three times, as fast as you can. It isn't as easy as you might think!

Letter Spotting

Write the letters of the alphabet down the side of a piece of paper. As you drive along, look for something beginning with each letter and write it down. The first to finish the alphabet wins.

Dots and Dashes

Draw a grid of horizontal and vertical dots, as shown below. The larger the grid, the longer the game will go on. Each take turns drawing a line connecting one dot with another, but not diagonally. The idea is to finally connect the dots into squares. The person that adds the last line of each square puts their initial in it, then they have another turn. The person with the most squares wins.

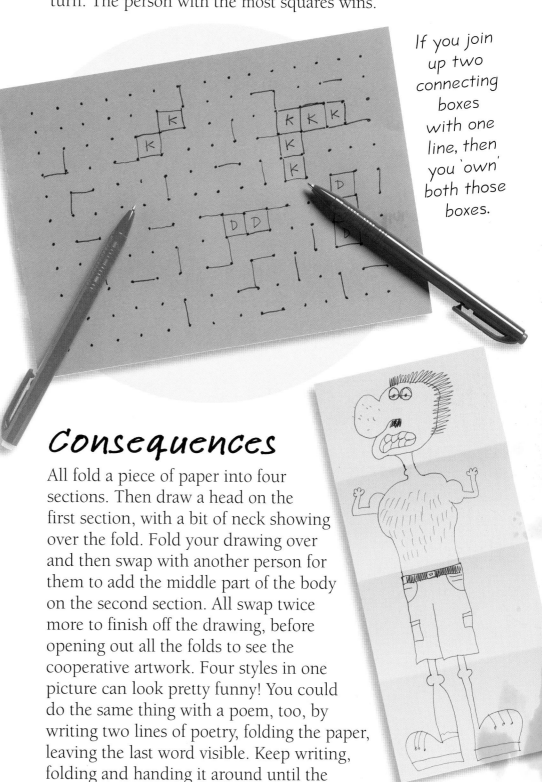

If you join up two connecting boxes with one line, then you 'own' both those boxes.

Consequences

All fold a piece of paper into four sections. Then draw a head on the first section, with a bit of neck showing over the fold. Fold your drawing over and then swap with another person for them to add the middle part of the body on the second section. All swap twice more to finish off the drawing, before opening out all the folds to see the cooperative artwork. Four styles in one picture can look pretty funny! You could do the same thing with a poem, too, by writing two lines of poetry, folding the paper, leaving the last word visible. Keep writing, folding and handing it around until the poem is finished.